J
597.8
Owe
Owen
Tadpole to frog

6912513
14.95

DATE DUE			

GREAT RIVER REGIONAL LIBRARY

St. Cloud, Minnesota 56301

GAYLORD M2G

LIFEWATCH

The Mystery of Nature

Tadpole to Frog

Oliver S. Owen

Published by Abdo & Daughters, 4940 Viking Drive, Suite 622, Edina, Minnesota 55435.

Library bound edition distributed by Rockbottom Books, Pentagon Tower, P.O. Box 36036, Minneapolis, Minnesota 55435.

Printed in the United States.

Cover Photo credit: Peter Arnold
Interior Photo credits: Animals Animals

Edited By Bob Italia

LIBRARY OF CONGRESS CATALOGING-IN-PUBLICATION DATA

Owen, Oliver S., 1920-
    Tadpole to Frog / Oliver S. Owen.
        p.   cm. -- (Lifewatch)
    Includes bibliographical references (p. 30) and index.
    ISBN 1-56239-291-3
    1. Frogs -- Juvenile literature. 2. Amphibians--Metamorphosis-
  -Juvenile literature.   I. Title. II. Series: Owen, Oliver S.,
  1920- Lifewatch.
    QL668.E2095   1995
    597.8'043--dc20   94-11370
                                              CIP
                                              AC

Contents

Frogs

Have you ever tried to catch a frog? Pretty tough, wasn't it? Or maybe, with one or two big hops, it made its escape into a pond. Frogs are amazing creatures. They belong to a large group of animals called amphibians (am-FIB-e-ans). There are roughly 2,700 different kinds the world over. They are found on every continent except Antarctica. About 155 kinds live in the United States and Canada. In Georgia's Okefenokee Swamp, there are millions of amphibians per square mile!

The word "amphibian" means "two lives." Most frogs can live either on land or in the water. Some frogs, however, live on land all the time. They may dig burrows in the ground with sharp little "spades" on the sides of their rear feet. They live in these burrows much of the time. Other kinds of frogs live mainly in trees. Sucking pads on their fingers and toes help them climb up trunks and branches. When they fall out of a tree, their spread-out fingers and toes act like little parachutes and slow down the frogs' fall to the ground.

Frogs vary greatly in size. The smallest frogs are only about a half inch long—about the size of your fingernail! The goliath frog of Africa, which is almost one foot long, is the world's largest.

Notice the sucking pads on the toes of this tree frog.

Frogs come in many shapes and sizes.

Frogs come in various colors. This is a red-bellied tree frog.

Frogs are beneficial to humans in many ways. They feed mostly on insects, many of which may be harmful to agricultural crops. For example, the cricket frog eats more than 5,000 insects a season. Certainly, frogs save farmers millions of dollars. The rear legs of large frogs are considered "good eating" by many people. Frogs are raised on "farms" in order to satisfy this demand. Biology students learn about body organs by dissecting frogs in the laboratory. They also study frog eggs under the microscope to learn about early development. Medical scientists inject new drugs into frogs to find out their effects.

The Adult Frog
The Body of the Frog

The frog has a short, chunky body. It lacks a tail. The frog's skin is smooth and moist. (Toads have much drier, warty skin.) The skin serves as an "outside" lung. Oxygen from the air passes through the skin to the inside of the frog. The eyes bulge out. This gives the frog a wide field of view. Just behind each eye is a round membrane which serves as an eardrum. It picks up sounds and sends them on as signals to the hearing part of the brain. The frog has no outer ears like humans do.

In many kinds of frogs, the male has a vocal sac at the bottom of the throat. It enlarges when the male frog is calling a female during the breeding season. This makes the call carry farther. The rear legs are long and muscular. The rear feet are webbed. This makes the rear limbs excellent organs for jumping and swimming. The front legs are short. They serve as shock absorbers when the frog hits the ground after each jump.

Notice the bulging eyes and ear membrane on this American bullfrog.

Food and Feeding Behavior

Many frogs feed mainly on insects with the help of a long sticky tongue. The tongue remains folded back inside the mouth until the frog spots a moving insect. Then suddenly the frog flicks out its tongue at the insect. This happens too fast for the human eye to follow! The insect gets stuck to the tongue as if it were flypaper! Then the tongue is withdrawn into the mouth. The insect is swallowed whole. A few kinds of frogs have no tongue. They simply scoop food into their mouths with their fingers.

This South American horned frog is eating a mouse.

Some toads feed on animals as large as mice! You say, "How in the world do they catch a fast animal like a mouse?" Well, this is how the horned toad from Asia does it. The back of the toad has a dark brownish-gray color. When about to feed, it burrows itself halfway in dead leaves. When a mouse gets close enough, the toad lunges forward and seizes the mouse with its jaws.

The common toad of Europe feeds on honey bees. It often sits at the entrance to a beehive. When a bee returns to the hive, it quickly winds up in the toad's stomach. Some frogs feed mainly on termites or "white ants." It makes sense for them to live inside a termite nest. And so they do! The American bullfrog has been known to feed on bats.

The writer dissected a bullfrog stomach and found two smaller frogs inside. They were caught while mating!

However, the African bullfrog gets the prize for an unusual meal. It quickly caught and ate 16 young cobra snakes it found in a zoo. The head end of a seventeenth cobra was in its stomach when the frog was finally discovered!

This American bullfrog is trying to eat a ribbon snake.

How Frogs Protect Themselves From Their Enemies

A few years ago, a scientist was walking along a Wisconsin lake. Suddenly he heard a pitiful scream. He hurried over to the sound. There he found a snake feeding on a frog. The rear legs of the frog had been swallowed. The head and trunk were still sticking out of the snake's mouth. Gradually the snake swallowed the entire frog.

Many kinds of animals would like to make a meal out of a frog. When frogs are out of the water, they have to be on the lookout for snakes, hawks, opossums, raccoons, skunks, and dogs. When in the water, frogs may be eaten by fish, turtles, waterfowl, wading birds, mink and otter. Small frogs may even be eaten by larger frogs. Frogs seem very defenseless. After all, they are rather small, weak and soft-bodied. With so many enemies, one would think the frog population would quickly go down to zero. Surprisingly, however, frogs can protect themselves in a number of interesting ways. Let's look at some of them.

Jumping Ability

The long, muscular hind legs of a frog are marvelous organs for jumping. Most frogs live only one leap or two from the edge of some pond, lake or stream. Perhaps the world's best jumper is a species from South Africa. This two-inch frog can jump 10 feet—60 times its body length. If you could do as well, you could easily jump half the length of a football field, or from third base to home plate!

Notice the long, muscular legs on this frog as it jumps into the water.

Protective Coloration

Many frogs are colored like their background. This is known as protective coloration. Frogs that live on the forest floor are often colored brown like the dead leaves all around them. Frogs that frequently climb trees are often colored like tree bark. Many of these tree frogs can actually change their color to gray, green or brown so that they more closely match the bark. Similarly, frogs that spend much of their time among marsh plants are often bright green. A hungry hawk, raccoon or fox might look right at such a frog without recognizing it as a possible meal!

Notice how the color of this frog blends in with the leaves.

Frightening Marks and Sounds

Some frogs have special markings on their bodies which tend to frighten hungry enemies away. They might have a pair of large dark "eye spots" on their rumps. When these frogs lower their heads and turn their backs, the fierce-looking "eyes" may cause the enemy to flee.

Many frogs will scream loudly when grabbed by another animal. This may startle it so much that it will drop the frog and let it escape.

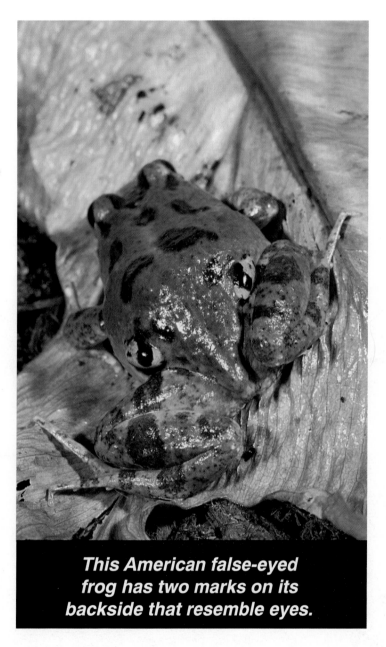

This American false-eyed frog has two marks on its backside that resemble eyes.

Unpleasant or Harmful Secretions

Many frogs have glands in their skin which make protective fluids. Have you ever been able to catch a frog—and hang on to it? Most likely it slipped out of your grasp because of the slippery mucus made by its skin glands. The pickerel frog, common in eastern United States, secretes a bad-tasting

The poison dart frog secretes a deadly mucus.

juice when seized by a dog or other animal. Often the dog will drop the frog rather than swallow such a horrible meal! In 1976, scientists discovered a bright orange frog in western Columbia. It was named the poison dart frog. Although only about one inch long, its skin glands produce enough poison to kill at least 20 people! The Choco Indians use this poison on the tips of their hunting darts. As you might expect, the poison dart frog has very few enemies.

Strange Body Shapes

Many frogs escape being eaten because they don't look like frogs! Their strange looks are caused by fleshy folds of skin which "decorate" different parts of their body. They may be "horns" above the eyes or flaps which stick out from the snout. Still other frogs may have fleshy frills on the outer edge of their arms, legs and ankles. In each case, these structures change the shape of the body. Therefore, a hungry frog-eater doesn't recognize the frog and moves on to find a meal some place else.

This tree frog has bumps all over its body, making it look unfriendly to its enemies.

Playing "Dead"

You probably have heard about opossums "playing dead" to escape enemies. Some frogs do a pretty good job of this as well. For example, when a tree frog falls to the ground, it may play dead for a minute or more. It will shut its eyes. It will draw its arms and legs close to the body. And it will make itself very stiff. If a nearby enemy feeds only on living frogs, this "playing dead" act may save the tree frog's life.

Use of Flash Colors

Some frogs are green or gray on top. However, the belly and underside of their legs are bright yellow, red or orange. Why should such color patches protect them from their enemies? Suppose that a raccoon finds such a frog which is resting. Its back blends with the grass. The raccoon lunges for the frog. The frog jumps away just in time. As it does so, the bright color of its underparts suddenly flashes. But then, as the frog comes down and folds its legs, the bright flash colors just as quickly disappear! Scientists believe that this sudden flash of color startles a predator and causes it to lose track of the frog. Then it will be forced to look elsewhere for its meal.

This monkey frog has a plain green back but its legs are bright orange which help to scare away enemies.

Reproduction

Frog reproduction is divided into the following parts: (1) territory of the male; (2) mating calls of the male; (3) the mating act and release of eggs and sperm; (4) the tadpole or polliwog; and (5) metamorphosis (met-uh-MOR-foe-sis) into a frog. Let's take a look at the reproductive behavior of the leopard frog, a common species in the United States.

Territory of the Male

In early spring, the male will establish a territory—an area which it will defend against other male leopard frogs. The territory is usually located in shallow water which has a few weeds. It may be two or three feet in diameter. The male will start calling from its territory. This call is a form of territorial defense. Most other male leopard frogs will stay away from the owner's territory when they hear this call. However, another male may invade the owner's territory.

Frogs will fight each other to protect their territory.

What will happen now? The owner will move straight at the invader and call more loudly and at a faster rate. This often causes the visitor to flee. The intruder may, however, hold its ground. This might result in a fight. The frogs have horns or spines. During a territorial fight, these structures may cause serious injury or even death.

The Mating Call

As we have seen, the call of the male keeps most other males out of the owner's territory. However, it also has another function. It attracts a female frog to the male's territory. However, it attracts only female frogs of the same kind as the caller. In fact, the females of some kinds of frogs are deaf to all mating calls except those of their own species.

Frog mating calls vary greatly from species to species. The leopard frog makes a croaking sound. You can imitate it by scratching a wet balloon! Some frogs have been named after their mating calls. The spring peeper, common in the United States, gives off high-pitched bird-like peeps. The American bullfrog sounds like the distant roaring of a bull. Close up it sounds like it is saying "jug-of-rum" over and over.

The mating call of the green frog sounds like the pluck of a guitar string. Some mating calls remind one of the whistling of the wind, the squeaking of a wagon wheel, or the sound made by a finger running over the teeth of a comb! If you are interested, you can get a record of frog calls and learn to identify the species.

Many kinds of male frogs have a vocal sac at the floor of the mouth. The frog forces air over its vocal cords and then into this sac so that it balloons outward and vibrates. This increases the loudness of the mating call so that some can be heard more than a mile away!

This reed frog has an inflated vocal sac.

The Mating Act

A female of the same species as the calling male will respond to its call. She will swim through the water to him. He will then hop on her back and hug her tightly with his arms. This is called the mating act. The female may carry the male on her back for some time while she swims through the water. Other males may try to dislodge the successful male from his perch. Usually, however, they do not succeed. The male will keep his grip on the female until she releases eggs. In the leopard frog, this may sometimes take several hours. The touch of the male's body sooner or later stimulates the female to release eggs.

Rain frogs in the mating act.

The number of eggs released varies from 19 to 30,000 eggs, depending on the species. As the eggs pass from the female's body, they are fertilized by sperm released by the male. In many species, the eggs form a string or a mat. The eggs may be attached to a water plant. In some species, the eggs are placed under a rock near the edge of the pond or stream. Some frogs produce eggs with a coating of thin jelly. The frogs move their feet back and forth through the egg mass until it forms a foam-like "nest." This "nest" may then float on the water.

Eggs of the rain frog. Notice the developing bodies inside.

In other species, eggs may be attached to a branch which hangs low over the pond. When these eggs hatch, the tiny tadpoles drop down into the water. The male European toad wraps the eggs around its legs. In yet another species, the eggs are placed on the back of the female. They gradually settle down into the skin and remain there until they hatch. In at least one kind of frog, the male injects sperm into the female's reproductive tract. Fertilization of the eggs takes place inside the female body. Some time later, it gives "birth" to tiny frogs.

The Tadpole

Most frogs are black on top and white below. The dark pigment soaks up warmth from the sun. This quickens the development of the embryo inside the egg. It lives on the food which is stored in the egg. Sooner or later it changes into a tadpole or polliwog. Depending on the kind of frog, it takes two to 30 days for the egg to hatch into a tadpole.

The tadpole is a small, fish-like stage of development. At first it cannot swim. The head of the tadpole is rather large. It has a pair of suckers on the chin. With these suckers, the tadpole can stick to water plants or twigs. Otherwise, it would fall into the mud at the bottom of the pond.

After a few days, the tadpole is able to swim. It does this by tail movements. Then the suckers are no longer needed and disappear. The tadpole has a pair of small eyes and a large mouth. The mouth is lined with rows of tiny tooth-like structures. With these "teeth," the tadpole shreds off bits of small water plants. These plants form its main food supply.

This is a photo of a frog embryo.

To digest these plants, the frog has a very long gut. It is coiled up like a watch spring. In some frogs, the larger tadpoles feed on smaller tadpoles. The tadpole breathes by means of gills. They take dissolved oxygen out of the water. This oxygen moves from the gill into the bloodstream. It is then carried throughout the tadpole's body.

The tadpole needs this oxygen to stay alive. In the older tadpole, the lungs form and the gills disappear. At this time, the tadpole must rise to the surface to gulp air which then passes to the lungs.

Metamorphosis

Sooner or later, the tadpole changes into a frog by a process called metamorphosis. This word means "change of form." The age of the tadpole at metamorphosis varies with the species. It may happen when the tadpole is only a couple weeks old. Or, as in the bullfrog, it may be three years before the tadpole changes into a frog. The changes are triggered by chemicals in the blood known as hormones.

The rear legs develop first. Some time later, the front legs form. About this same time, the gills are lost and lungs develop in their place. The tadpole must now rise to the surface to gulp air. The skeleton hardens. Jaws develop. The tiny tooth-like structures are replaced by real teeth. The shape of the head becomes more frog-like. The tadpole's intestine shortens and becomes suited to digest insects.

The gray tree frog tadpole.

Brown-striped frog with tadpole features. Notice the tail of a tadpole but legs and head of a frog.

After several days of dramatic changes, the tadpole has at last become a frog! Only the stub of a tail is left to show it once was a tadpole. And that soon disappears.

In a few kinds of frogs, metamorphosis is completed inside the egg. The eggs hatch directly into tiny frogs! Some frogs in the American tropics lay their eggs on land. After the eggs hatch, the male frogs carry the little tadpoles on their back to some nearby stream. Still more unusual is the tadpole-carrying method of the mouth-breeding frog of South America. The male takes up the eggs in its mouth. Then they pass into its vocal sac where they first hatch into tadpoles and then change into frogs. A short time later, the tiny frogs leave the vocal sac and hop out of the male's mouth!

Frogs have many different ways of breeding and developing. But in most of the world's frogs, breeding is much the same. The young frogs grow up to be adult. Males set up their territories and call the females. Mating takes place. Eggs are fertilized by the male and develop into tadpoles. They, in turn, undergo metamorphosis and change into young frogs. It's an amazing story, don't you think?

Glossary

Amphibian   a smooth, moist-skinned animal that at some time breathes with external gills and is suited as an adult for both life on land and in water.

Flash colors bright color patches on a frog's body which it flashes to confuse an animal that might eat it.

Gills   soft, membranous structures that the tadpole uses to get oxygen from the water.

Hormone   a chemical made by a gland that enters the bloodstream and plays a role in metamorphosis.

Metamorphosis the series of body changes in a tadpole as it develops into an adult frog.

Species   a kind of animal or plant.

Tadpole   the stage of a frog between the egg and adult.

Territory   an area that is defended by a frog against other members of its species.

Vocal sacs   sack-like structures on the floor of the frog's mouth that increase the carrying capacity of the voice.

Bibliography

Mattison, Christopher. *Frogs and Toads of the World.* New York: Facts on File, 1987.

Smith, Hobart M. *Amphibians of North America.* New York: Golden Press, 1978.

Vogt, Richard Carl. *Natural History of Amphibians and Reptiles of Wisconsin.* Milwaukee: Milwaukee Public Museum, 1981.

Wright, Albert and Anna Wright. *Handbook of Frogs and Toads of the United States.* Ithaca, New York: Comstock Publishing Company, 1949.

Index

A

African bullfrog 9
American bullfrog 9, 19
amphibians 4
Antarctica 4

B

branches 4
breeding 7, 27
bright flash 16
bullfrog 9, 19, 25
burrows 4, 8

C

Canada 4
Choco Indians 14
cobra 9
cricket frog 6

D

defense 10, 18

E

eggs 6, 17, 21, 22, 23, 27
embryo 23
European toad 23
eye spots 13

F

fertilization 23

G

gills 24, 25, 28
goliath frog 4

H

hormones 25
horned toad 8
horns 15, 19

I

insects 6, 8, 25

L

leopard frog 17, 18, 19, 21

M

marsh plants 12
mating 9, 17, 19, 20, 21
metamorphosis 17, 25, 27, 28

N

nest 9, 22

O

Okefenokee Swamp 4
oxygen 24, 25

P

parachutes 4
pickerel frog 14
poison dart frog 14
polliwog 17, 23
protective coloration 12

R

reproduction 17, 23

S

skin glands 14
species 11, 17, 19, 20, 21, 22, 23, 25
sperm 17, 22, 23
spring peeper 19
sucking pads 4

T

tadpole 17, 23, 24, 25, 27
territory 17, 18, 19, 29
tongue 8
tree frogs 16
trunks 4

U

United States 4, 14, 17, 19

V

vocal sac 7, 20, 27

About the Author

Oliver S. Owen is a Professor Emeritus for the University of Wisconsin at Eau Claire. He is the coauthor of *Natural Resource Conservation: An Ecological Approach* (Macmillan, 1991). Dr. Owen has also authored *Eco-Solutions* and *Intro to Your Environment* (Abdo & Daughters, 1993). Dr. Owen has a Ph.D. in zoology from Cornell University.

To my grandson, Amati,
may you grow up to always
appreciate and love nature.
— Grandpa Ollie